Josh Kraus
Chicago, IL 60607
http://www.IsThisAcidInMyApplesauce.com

Kraus, Josh, 1989 –
Is This Acid In My Applesauce? / by Josh Kraus; illustrated by Daryl Alexsy
1st ed.
p.cm.
Summary: Is This Acid In My Applesauce? is a twisted tale for grownups about a little boy who feeds his head with more than just junk food.
ISBN 978-0-615-89740-0 (ebook)
[1. Monsters – Fiction. 2. Adventure – Fiction. 3. Imagination – Fiction. 4. Humor – Fiction. 5. Illustration – Fiction.]

For the kid in all of us, and the parent in all of us, and the tacos
in all of us.

CHAPTER ONE: THEO

"**MOM** dad mom dad mom dad! Did you know that koala bears hug each other when they're sad? Nah just kidding they poop and pee and fart like all the other animals!"

Theo rambled when he was excited, and today he was pumped to the max. His grandparents just moved into a new house, and apparently they bought a giant trampoline for him to play on. Yeah, a GIANT TRAMPOLINE!

But mom was driving *so* slow. Didn't she understand? Out of all the things you could jump on, trampolines were definitely the bounciest. Way bouncier than hotel beds or pogo sticks or dad's face. *I think when moms get older they forget to bounce on stuff. That must be why they drive so slow.* Theo was always smart for his age.

"Well hello there!" Granddad said after Theo and his parents *finally* arrived.

"Just look at this handsome family," Grandma added. "You in particular Mister Theodore."

Theo always hated when people called him that, but he still gave Grandma and Granddad big hugs. He would give a million hugs for a jump on the trampoline.

"Where is it Grandma?" Theo asked longingly. "How high will it bounce me? Could I high five a bird? What kind of bird though? A space bird?"

Grandma laughed. "You'll just have to find out. It's in the basement, but it's a mess down there so be careful."

Theo started toward the stairs.

"NOT YET," his mother's voice boomed. "Do you remember what I told you young man?"

Theo sighed. "I need to help Grandma and Granddad unpack before I can play."

"You can help put the books away," Grandma offered.

Theo groaned. *Old people books.*

"And the dishes," Granddad said.

Old people dishes.

Grandma winked at him. "But I baked cupcakes …"

*Cupcakes? Cupcakes aren't bouncy! Nice try Granny, but I won't forget about the trampoline **that** easily.*

I hope she remembered sprinkles though.

Sprinkles are awesome.

CHAPTER TWO: CURT & DEB

"JESUS THEO, quit bouncing around back there!" Deb shouted as they swerved into the driveway. "This is how Bambi died!" Theo didn't seem to hear her.

"Huh, that usually works," Curt said. "The lure of a giant trampoline must be too powerful."

"Why did you even tell him about the You-Know-What?" she murmured. "That's like catnip for kids his age."

"For the last time Deb, don't compare him to a cat. Contrary to what the internet would have you believe, cats are the sociopaths of the animal kingdom. Theo's more like a lemur, bouncing and swinging and–"

"Throwing his poop at the mailman?"

Curt sighed. "Give him a break. I feel like you're forgetting all the times he *didn't* throw his poop at the mailman."

"Hello people," Granddad grunted.

"Trampoleeeeen trampoleeeeen gahhhhhh!"

Granddad nodded in Curt's direction. "I think I smell hooch on that boy's breath."

"I'll get right on that Dad," Curt said, rolling his eyes.

"Curt my boy, I need to have a serious discussion with you," Granddad continued. "Did you know the FBI has blueprints for a penis-shaped roller coaster that they don't want you to know about?!"

During this exchange of pleasantries, Deb was reminding Theo that he could only play with the trampoline once he helped his grandparents unpack.

"Do you remember what I told you Theo?"

Theo frowned. "I dunno, put stuff away or something."

His grandparents tried to cheer him up, but Theo's pouty little scowl stayed put. *Your life is so hard, isn't it?* Deb thought. *You're a little white suburban boy living in a country where you can buy gluten free baby food. Get over it.*

"I baked cupcakes …" Grandma said.

Classic Granny move. Why didn't I think of that? Deb looked at Theo.

Poof, all smiles. Maybe parenting wasn't that hard after all.

CHAPTER THREE: THEO

WHILE a perfectly bouncy trampoline was waiting to be bounced on, Theo had to help his grandparents put all the stupid dishes in the stupid cupboard. Then he had to put all the stupid books on the stupid bookshelf. Nothing had ever been this boring, or stupid. Dumb stupid chores!

He couldn't stand it anymore. He needed entertainment! Theo scanned the room. No roller coasters, no action figures, no submarines, no sandboxes, no pirate ships, no squirt guns, no regular guns, no robot sharks, no crayons, no nuthin! Just books and boxes and dad's coat. Wait ... dad's coat!

When no one was looking, Theo rifled through the coat pockets, hoping to find something cool to play with.

He grabbed the car keys and pretended he was Wolverine.

He grabbed his dad's wallet and pretended he was an FBI detective.

He popped a gum wrapper into his mouth and pretended he was a cowboy chewin' tobakkee.

But Granddad put an end to his adventures and herded him back into the kitchen.

"What were you doing back there son?"

"Just saving the world and stuff."

Granddad chuckled. "You were always a crazy kid. Do you still cry and wave goodbye to your poop when you flush it?"

"It's cuz I'll never see it again!"

"We played around too when I was your age. Marbles, kick the can, leap frog. Sometimes we'd shine a flashlight behind our fingers and if they glowed red it meant you were a DIRTY STINKIN COMMIE!"

Granddad wasn't making any sense, but he kept on blabbering while Theo returned to book duty. Books! The one thing in the world you couldn't have fun with. This was going to be a long, unbouncy day.

CHAPTER FOUR: CURT & DEB

WHILE a perfectly good Antiques Roadshow marathon was nearing an end, Curt and Deb had to carefully position each piece of furniture in the spot where it would, according to Curt's mother, "offer the most protection against mudslides and zoo animal escapes" – two things which coincidentally had been on the news recently.

"Why isn't your brother here?" Deb whispered to Curt. "We'd be done by now."

"Tim is hosting what he likes to call a 'spirit circle' in his backyard sweat lodge. He said he would 'be here in spirit' and then laughed and hung up."

"That doped up lunatic, of course he did. Well then where are the car keys? I think I left my phone in the cupholder."

Translation: *I can't stand your mother, I need some fresh air, and I'm considering faking my own death and starting a new life as a corn maze designer in Nebraska.* Curt could be paranoid at times.

"I bet Theo has the keys," Deb said to herself. "He's like a cat when it comes to jangly metal."

"Again with the cat! LEMUR Deb."

Deb went in search of her son and returned moments later with the keys and a small scrap of foil in her hand.

"Curt, what's this? I found it in Theo's pocket with the keys. A gum wrapper? He has a fructose intolerance Curt!"

"And yet you let him eat cupcakes," Curt muttered. He fingered the bit of tinfoil curiously, then froze. "Oh balls."

CHAPTER FIVE: THEO

THEO was sure Grandma had forgotten the sprinkles, but there it was, one little orange sprinkle right in the palm of his hand. It was so tiny and alone.

You never see just one sprinkle. One sprinkle is useless. It's like only having one ball in a ball pit. Or just one wish from a genie. He wondered what the magic number of sprinkles was. *20? 30? Oh gee ... 40? COULD IT BE 40 SPRINKLES?!* There was so much about the world he didn't know, and sprinkle ratios were just the beginning.

WHAT WAS THE OPPOSITE OF A SANDWICH?

COULD I JUST BITE INTO THE STRING CHEESE INSTEAD OF PEELING IT?

IF I HAD TO POOP AND THEN TRAVELLED BACK IN TIME, WOULD I NOT HAVE TO POOP ANYMORE?

"Anyone home?" Granddad tapped Theo's shoulder. "You day dreaming son?"

"Granddad I need to know about time travel pooping!"

Granddad got serious. "If you're a time traveller, always make sure to bring a chain wallet so that no matter what year you're in, people will know you mean business."

Theo nodded solemnly.

"Now sober up boy! We've got some appliances to unload. There's the coffee maker, the blender, the toaster, the I'll-never-let-you-go-on-the-trampoline mixer, the rice cooker..."

That's right, the trampoline! He had almost forgotten. Suddenly a terrifying thought occurred to him.

WHAT IF THEY NEVER LET ME JUMP ON IT?

WHAT IF THOSE CUPCAKES WERE MADE FROM MURDERED TRAMPOLINE BABIES?

WHAT IF I CAN NEVER GROW A SWEET MUSTACHE?

He needed to see that trampoline, and he needed to see it now. Quietly, Theo backed out of the kitchen and was only halfway through the living room when he heard his parents approaching. *You guys might play hide-and-seek, but I live it.* And with that he dove under a pile of cardboard boxes.

CHAPTER SIX: CURT & DEB

"**SHIT.** How ... but ... oh god. Shit Deb, shit shit shitty shit shit SHIT!" Curt was pacing the room and starting to sweat.

"Shhhh!" Deb whispered. "Maybe it was sugarless."

"No Deb you don't get it."

"Get what? What Curt!"

Curt was biting his nails, something he only did when he was reading horoscopes on the morning of a doctor's appointment, or when he had a bunch of Cheeto dust on his fingers.

"This can't be happening," Curt said. "I *never* do anything this stupid. No seriously. I don't text and drive, I won't reach into the garbage disposal, I've never googled '*analogy*' because it's too close to 'anal orgy' –"

"CURT TELL ME WHAT HAPPENED!"

"Ok but the most important thing to remember Deb, above everything else, is that –"

"Everyone is ok?"

"–it technically isn't my fault, could've happened to anyone really –"

"CURTIS!"

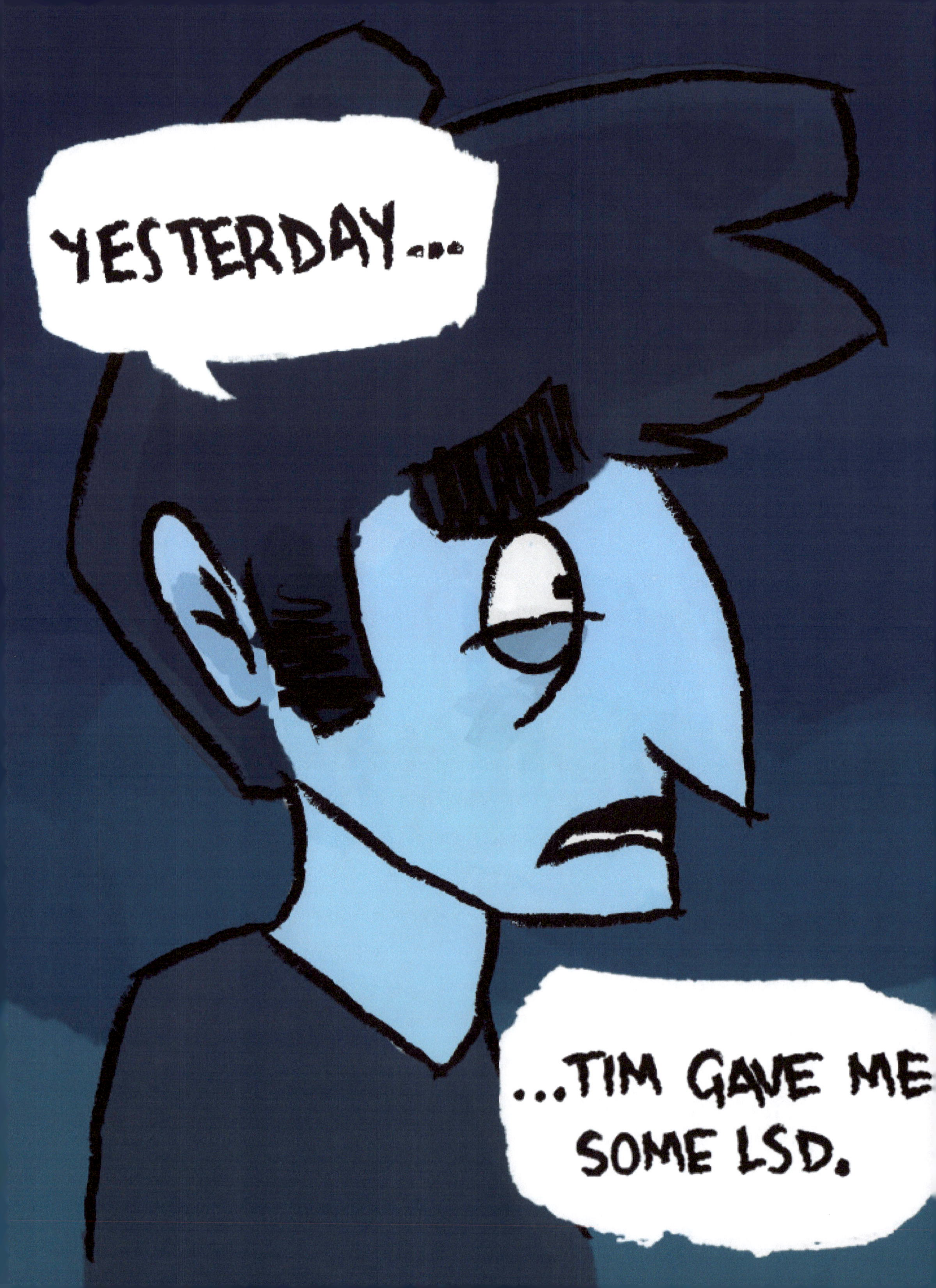
YESTERDAY...
...TIM GAVE ME SOME LSD.

CHAPTER SEVEN: THEO

BOX wouldn't shut up and Theo was getting worried that his parents might hear.

"I'm sorry Box, you know I am," Theo whispered. "But I can't play spaceship with you right now. I can't play dinosaur rider or gas station attendant or pineapple salesman either. Things are different now that there's a trampoline I can play on."

"Why would you want to do that?" Box asked. "Don't go, stay with Box. Box is your friend. Box … loves you Theo."

"Did you love me when you gave me that papercut last year at Roger's birthday party? That hurt!"

"Oh Theo we were just playing, that's all."

"No, you were mad because I ditched you for that swing set."

WHACK! Suddenly Box exploded and Theo was out in the open. Someone was coming for him. Grandma? Evil Theo? Time-travelling Granddad? Jeez first the sprinkles and now this. Heckuva day for a five-year-old.

But it wasn't over yet. The ghastly figure was getting closer. It screeched like a seagull singing karaoke. It was holding that icky gum in it's hand that had tasted like a zipper. Whatever it planned on doing, it certainly didn't involve jumping on trampolines. *It's now or never*, Theo thought, and he bolted toward the basement.

This is it. Freedom! Trampolines! Jumping on things! Theo was nearly at the bottom of the stairs when the monster tried to eat him.

He was looking at a gazillion slimy tentacles and a mouth big enough to fit a plus-sized gopher. Its eyes were cold and empty and its breath smelled like a million butts.

Theo turned to run but the hideous beast had grabbed him, its gaping mouth opening wider and wider. *I can't get eaten,* Theo thought. *That would be so gross.* He twisted and pulled and stomped on the monster's foot. Finally he wriggled through its grasp and sprinted back upstairs.

"Theodore what's wrong dear?" someone asked.

"Tell everyone to get out while they still can!" Theo yelled. "THERE'S A MONSTER AND IT TRIED TO EAT ME!" *How could they have bought a house without making absolutely sure there were no monsters in it? Dummies.*

CHAPTER EIGHT: CURT & DEB

"CURT where's your boy?" his father shouted from the kitchen. "I was told he'd be cheap labor!"

"You know what LSD is, right Curtis?" Deb said, not taking her eyes off her husband.

Curt nodded meekly.

"And Tim, your dumbass, deadbeat, hippie-dippie shithead of a brother gave it to you *why* exactly?"

Deb looked at her husband of seven years and quietly congratulated herself for not punching him in the face. "If our baby boy really is on ... hallucinogens," she growled, "we are in serious trouble. He just learned how to tie his shoes Curt! This is how super villains are born Curt! What if he decides *today* is the day to play 'the floor is lava!'"

"Well how do we know he actually put it in his mouth? Theo! THEO! Dammit where is he?" Curt did a 360 of the room before he gave up and kicked a pile of cardboard boxes in frustration.

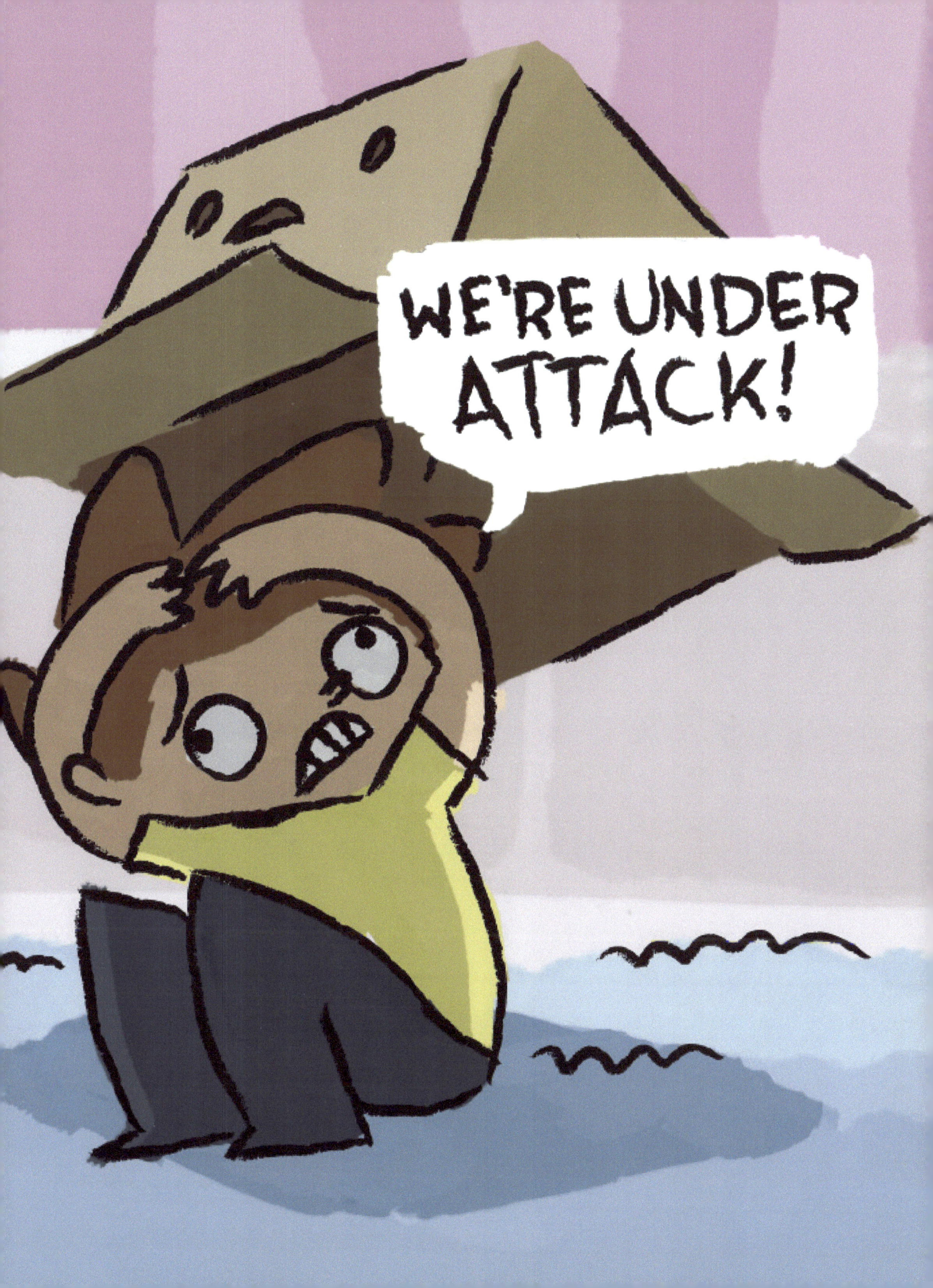
WE'RE UNDER ATTACK!

"Great Curt, way to dropkick your son in the face. That'll go over well when this inevitably goes to trial," Deb rushed toward her son and held out her hand. "Theo honey, I need you to look at this. Did you put this in your mouth?"

"It tasted like a zipper!" Theo shouted. Curt started mentally compiling a plea for joint-custody.

"Ok let's pump his stomach," Curt said. "Do we have a plunger or something?"

"How did he find it?" Deb hissed. "When did he take it? Oh god this isn't happening."

"I guess he took it out of my wallet after I hung up my coat. The acid was right behind my $25 Chili's gift card. Thanks again for that by the way. You're so kind and thoughtful -"

"*So* not the time."

"Totally. You're so good at knowing the right times for things honey."

"My guess is that Theo probably found the tab about 45 minutes ago. Right?"

"Maybe, why?"

"Because that means ..."

Grandma shuffled into the room. "Theodore looks a little under the weather Curt. Was it my cupcakes honey? Too many sprinkles I bet."

"What?" Curt jumped in front of Theo like he was guarding an unwrapped Christmas present. "No, I mean yes, yes I think he's feeling ill. The legal kind of ill obviously. I think we need to go home actually and –"

Without warning Theo bolted toward the basement, cackling loudly to himself as if no one could hear. He was gone for only a few seconds before careening wildly back into view.

Deb was grateful for Theo's constant state of motion, which made it much more difficult for his grandparents to notice that, thanks to his Oreo-sized pupils and flapping tendrils of drool, Theo really did look like a lemur. A rabid, fiending, lobotomized lemur. Curt would be so proud.

CHAPTER NINE: THEO

AFTER his parents rushed him out the door and sped back home (leaving poor old Grandma and Granddad to fend for themselves), Theo found himself pacing back and forth, deep in thought.

The trampoline drama seemed so silly now that there was monster drama, and he had run away like a big wuss! When he told everyone at school about the monster, which he'd have to because monster sightings were big news, they would all laugh at how he chickened out. *Scaredy butt! Monster wimp! Couldn't handle one little bloodthirsty beast!*

Being made fun of would be even worse than getting eaten, so there was only one choice: Be the coolest, toughest, most awesomest kid in the whole universe and charge into the monster's lair and slay the evil creature.

Then I'd have the craziest story to tell my friends and everyone at school will think I'm a superhero. Oh and Grandma and Granddad won't get eaten. That's good too I guess.

But Theo had never fought a whole monster before. Sure, he had wrestled garden hoses and won some pretty tough underwater kung-fu battles, but that wasn't the same. He needed to be at his monster-fighting prime, and to do that, Theo had to undergo Monster Combat Training.

CHAPTER TEN: CURT & DEB

"**MAYBE** I should call Tim and ask him how long this will last," Curt suggested once they were back home. "Like, what strength is this LSD. Mild? Medium?"

"It's not a plate of buffalo wings Curtis!" Deb spat. "I seriously can't believe you were going to take LSD. You're a 41-year-old computer programmer!"

"HERO TIME!" Theo shouted.

"What's he talking about Curt? Is that the drugs or just five-year-old gibberish. I can't tell!"

"I don't know. Nothing a five-year-old has ever said has ever made sense. EVER!"

Deb closed her eyes, took a few deep breaths, and said: "Theo's probably got about seven more hours until it leaves his system. We need to give him a safe space, put on some soothing nature sounds, and try to give him an environment where he can make a self-discovery."

"Self-discovery? What, that there's no little man in the crosswalk light? That all matter harmonizes?"

Deb's momentary calm shattered. "No, more like that his father is mayor of fuck nuts mountain and the reason he isn't around is because he's serving time for child endangerment and possession of a schedule one illegal drug! That's in the same class as heroin, fuck nuts, by the way."

"At least I'm not the one dropping enough F bombs around our five-year-old to flatten Tehran!"

"That's racist Curt!"

Just then the phone rang.

MONSTER COMBAT TRAINING!

DISCOVER THE ANCIENT ART OF KICKING A MONSTER IN ITS FAT STUPID FACE!

CHAPTER ELEVEN: THEO

LEARN TO DISEMBOWEL FIVE DIFFERENT SPECIES OF GOBLIN!

KNOW IN ADVANCE WHEN A MONSTER IS REALLY A METAPHOR FOR THE MONSTER WITHIN ALL OF US!

KILL A MONSTER WITH KINDNESS...AND CHAINSAWS!

ON DAY 1 OF MONSTER COMBAT TRAINING, THEO LEVELED UP ON SPEED. MONSTERS WERE USUALLY BIG AND SLOW, SO THEO NEEDED TO BE ABLE TO DART, ZOOM, AND SPRINT LIKE A CHEETAH WITH A JETPACK.

ON DAY 2 OF MONSTER COMBAT TRAINING,
THEO PUT ON SOME SERIOUS MUSCLE. MONSTERS WERE
PRETTY MUCH MADE OF SLIME AND BICEPS, SO THEO
NEEDED TO GET CRAZY BUILT, AND FAST.

ON DAY 3 OF MONSTER COMBAT TRAINING, THEO PRACTICED NOT BEING A TOTAL WUSS. EVERYONE KNEW THAT MONSTERS WERE ALLERGIC TO TOUGHNESS, SO THEO NEEDED TO GET RIPPED WITH BRAVERY.

CHAPTER TWELVE: CURT & DEB

"BAD NEWS," Deb said, hanging up. "That was your dad. We need to go back and move the table out of the garage so he can drive to the pharmacy."

As Curt met this new crisis, a strange calm washed over him and he felt the pieces of his mind align like pez in a pez dispenser. A wind of omnipotence blew through him and opened a gateway to his inner consciousness, and now he was seeing, *really* seeing. *This must be a contact high,* Curt thought. *I've heard of tales of this sorcery.* Everything shimmered under a golden light of total comprehension. All matter harmonized. He knew the answer. With a voice like smooth thunder, Curt announced:

"We will take the boy to the hospital."

"Child services," Deb replied.

"What if I go to my parents' house and you stay with Theo?"

"You're going to move a granite table by yourself?" Deb cried. "And if your mom or dad tries to help then we *will* have to go to a hospital. Or a funeral."

"Call a babysitter?"

"And never get a babysitter again? Theo is BATSHIT right now!"

"We could leave him here," Curt said desperately. "Lock the doors, put on the TV."

"He can't even watch a Blue's Clues rerun without racing around the house and screaming the names of appliances. And now he's on drugs! He could get violent."

"Yeah Deb, that episode where Blue had to figure out who viciously murdered Steve and left his mutilated body in the bathtub was pretty dark."

"I'm serious!"

"We have to leave him here Deb."

"We can't leave him here alone, there are too many mirrors!"

"Well we can't take him BACK to my mom and dad's." Curt's voice cracked with indignation. "I may not know a lot about drugs Deb, I get it. I don't have a cool job either and I've never been on a road trip and I don't have a pony tail or a tattoo of a butterfly over my heart. But I think I understand what *hallucinogenic properties* means.

It means our son will think we're a pair of evil overlords delivering him to some child eating demon monster.

He'll think his grandparents are former children whose souls were devoured and are now walking husks of withered flesh.

And god knows what will happen if he finds that trampoline. It's like a bouncy black hole of death!"

"Not to mention," he continued, "returning to the scene of the crime could adversely affect any synaesthesia, temporary dissociation, ego death, what Timothy Leary describes as 'set and setting,' and, well, there's probably more but the internet is being really slow right now."

"Curt, honey, look at our son. He's terrified of that pineapple fridge magnet. He's trying to impale his stuffed animals with a broom. He's making toast with WHOLE WHEAT BREAD! We have to keep an eye on him or else who knows what could happen. And unless you also want to google 'how to convince a court that giving your child LSD and leaving him at home alone to watch TV is not a punishable offense,' I suggest we leave, right now."

CHAPTER THIRTEEN: THEO, CURT & DEB

THEO arrived at his Grandparents' house ready to pound that butt-smelling freak into the ground.

"There's my Theodore," someone said. Grandma? It *was* Grandma, and Granddad too! They looked more wrinkly than usual, but other than that they were still uneaten. Phew.

"You're lucky I'm here," Theo announced. "Any minute longer and you might have been monster food. Outtah my way mortals!" And with that he charged toward the basement.

Curt ran after Theo, Deb ran after Curt, Grandma and Granddad shuffled slightly forward and then complained about their knees.

From the moment Theo came slip 'n sliding out of the womb, Curt had loved that little potato sack with the Gilbert Gottfried face as much as all those smug dad bloggers said he would. Theo grew up to be smart and adventurous and, yeah, occasionally batshit, but that was ok with Curt, even if it wasn't with Deb, because guess what?

Theo was just a kid for Christ's sake! Parents always forget that they used to be *just* as batshit as the kids they now supposedly "didn't understand" or thought "were exposed to too much K-Pop while in utero." But Theo on drugs? *Psychedelic* drugs? If he was usually normal kid crazy, what was he capable of now?

Theo took the steps two at a time, turned the corner, and came face to face with the horrible beast.

OBJECTIVE: **DESTROY BUTT SMELLING CREATURE.**
OFFENSIVE STRATEGY: **HIT IT WITH THINGS.**
DEFENSIVE STRATEGY: **(SEE OFFENSIVE STRATEGY).**
FINISHING MOVE: **STAB IT WITH WITH SOMETHING STABBY.**

"My name is *Theo*, and words can't save you now demon spawn!" Theo grabbed one of Granddad's golf clubs and catapulted off the trampoline. It was dark in the basement, but Theo's aim was true, and he lanced the monster right in the face. The beast stumbled backward and crashed into a shelf. A can of red paint tumbled off, splattering everything in sight.

Deb arrived at what appeared to be a bloody crime scene. She looked for Theo and saw him step over Curt and start battering an old coatrack with his tiny fists.

So that's what started it all. This old forgotten coatrack, easily dismissed as trash, has become a symbol for Theo's fear of aging, of becoming expendable. The coat rack must have triggered a profound hallucination representing a crisis of self, a loss of innocence, a sad triumph of responsibility over personal freedom. The monster is ... adulthood. My philosophy degree ... was worth the crippling debt after all.

The monster was on the ground, its entrails scattered around the room like piñata candy. Theo towered over his enemy, grinning fiercely. "You want some mayonnaise monster? Because you're about to get a knuckle sandwich ... WITH THE CRUSTS STILL ON IT!"

"What in god's pajamas is going on down there!" Curt's mother shouted as she hobbled down the steps.

"Stay upstairs!" Deb bellowed, but Grandma didn't listen. It was the slippery paint that got her in the end, and that afternoon Grandma flew high enough to headbutt an eagle. Except instead of an eagle she landed on Deb's face.

Curt barely heard the crash. In front of him, Theo was standing over the wooden shards of a broken coat rack, looking ready to pounce. *Mother of god, the splinters* was all Curt had time to think before scrambling toward his son.

Theo was going in for the kill when two pale tentacles grabbed him from behind. *Not a chance monster pants.* He gripped the stabby thing he had found in the corner and plunged it into the creature's neck.

"What happened to you people!" Curt's father shouted from his armchair. "Is that my insulin?"

"Theo …" Curt panted. "The – the coat rack."

"Oh right, that old coat rack. You think that's what scared him? Pansy."

"What's wrong with that boy!" screeched Curt's mother as she and Deb limped into the room. "It's those awful video games. And the skateboarders!"

"It's done," a voice said.

They all turned to see Theo standing by the stairs wearing Granddad's fake green beret and a strip of Grandma's fur coat hanging around his neck like a carcass.

"You're all safe now thanks to me and my super awesome monster fighting skills," Theo declared. "You should have seen me down there! I was all like **KERSMASHHHH** and the monster was like *GAHHHH* and then I went *KABANGGGG* and it went *ARGGGG* *SPLATTT* and then I was like..."

Curt's parents looked from Theo to Curt and Deb as if they expected a reasonable explanation. As Deb started stuffing cupcakes in Curt's mouth to raise his blood sugar, she tried to think of an excuse. PTSD, oxygen allergies, K-Pop – anything woud be better than admitting the truth. Suddenly her phone vibrated. It was a text.

1 new message received
Acid? Seriously Tim? This is NOT FUNNY!
TIM: did Curty actually take it? is he cheesin'? it wasn't acid, Deb, relax just part of a gum wrapper but please please please take a video! Namaste.

Deb turned to Curt's parents. "We think it might be ADD."

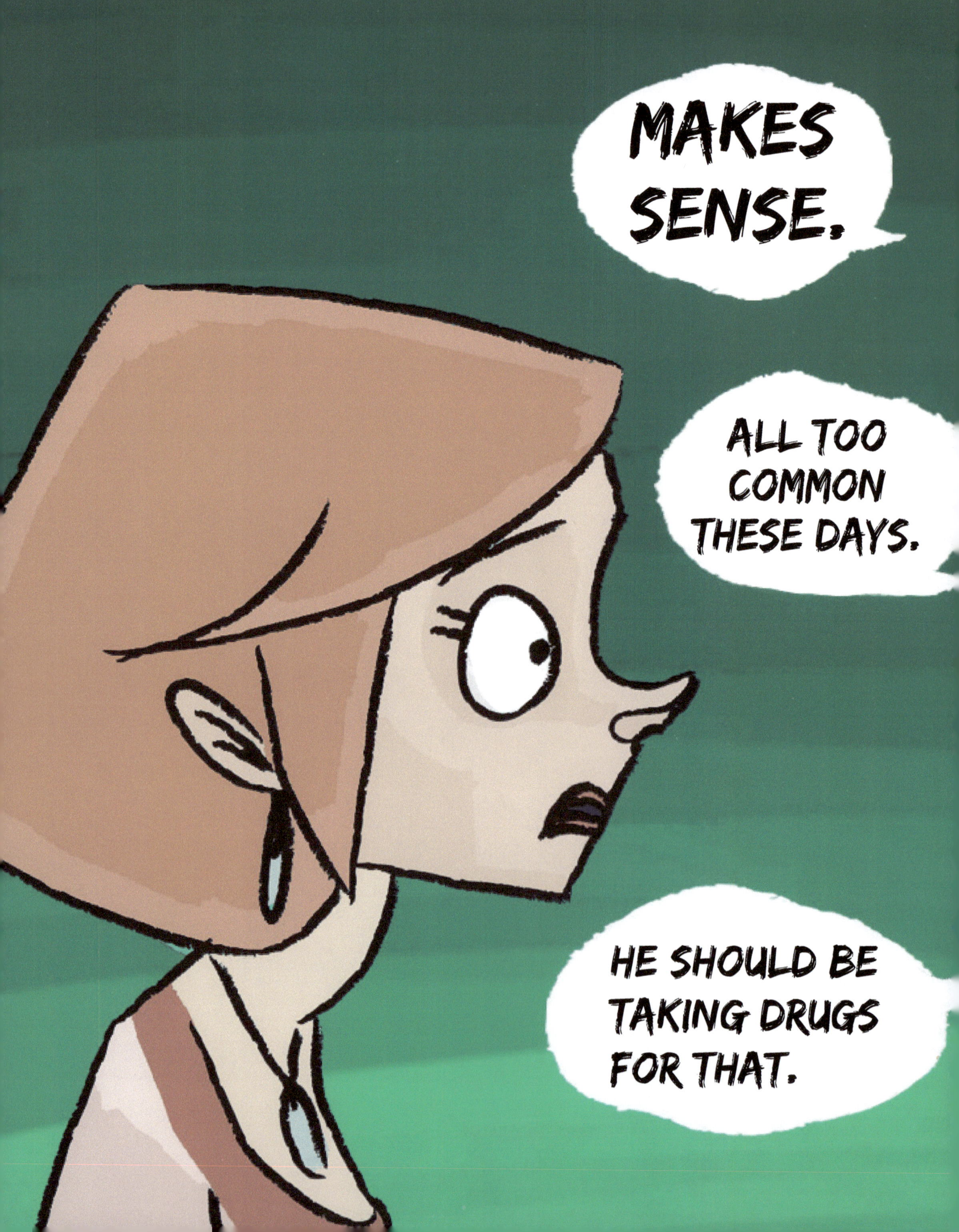

THE END

ACKNOWLEDGEMENTS

I'd like to thank the following people for sacrificing their time, energy, and the occasional unblemished lamb to help bring this book to life. You guys seriously rock.

Robbie Balan

Danielle Fleischman

Daniela Parra

Mom

Dad

Jamie Kraus

Bruno

BEWARE OF DOG!